Self-Discipline Mastery

Control your mind, build willpower & master your mindset.

Learn habits to overcome procrastination, increase self-confidence and develop mental toughness.

© Copyright 2019 - All rights reserved.

The content contained within this book may not be reproduced, duplicated, or transmitted without direct written permission from the author or the publisher.

Under no circumstances will any blame or legal responsibility be held against the publisher, or author, for any damages, reparation, or monetary loss due to the information contained within this book, either directly or indirectly.

Legal Notice:
This book is copyright protected. It is only for personal use. You cannot amend, distribute, sell, use, quote, or paraphrase any part, or the content within this book, without the consent of the author or publisher.

Disclaimer Notice:
Please note the information contained within this document is for educational and entertainment purposes only. All effort has been executed to present accurate, up-to-date, reliable, complete information. No warranties of any kind are declared or implied. Readers acknowledge that the author is not engaging in the rendering of legal, financial, medical, or professional advice. The content within this book has been derived from various sources. Please consult a licensed professional before attempting any techniques outlined in this book.

By reading this document, the reader agrees that under no circumstances is the author responsible for any losses, direct or indirect, that are incurred as a result of the use of the information contained within this document, including, but not limited to, errors, omissions, or inaccuracies.

Table of Contents

INTRODUCTION 5

PART 1: THEORY 9

CHAPTER 1: CONQUER YOUR MIND, CONQUER THE WORLD 11
   UNDERSTANDING SELF-DISCIPLINE 12
      What Is Self-Discipline 12
      Developing Your Self-Discipline 15
      Self-Confidence Vs. Self-Esteem 18

CHAPTER 2: MINDSET 25
   FIXED AND GROWTH MINDSET 29
      It Is Always Your Choice 29
      Fixed Mindset 30
      Growth Mindset 32
   TO LEARN OR NOT TO LEARN? 34
      Understand the World 34
      Teach Other People About Your World 36
      Treat Learning as an Inspiration 37
      Learning Helps Your Mindset Grow 38

CHAPTER 3: KEY TO SUCCESS 41
   MOTIVATED TO LEARN 45
   GROW YOUR MENTAL TOUGHNESS 48
      Core Distinctions of Mental Toughness 50
      Benefits of Mental Toughness 51

PART 2: PRACTICE 57

CHAPTER 4: THINK BIG, START SMALL 59
   GOLDEN GOAL SETTING RULES 61
      Write Down Your Goals 61
      Use the SMART Rule 62
      Your Goals Need to Keep You Motivated 65
   CREATING AN ACTION PLAN 66

CHAPTER 5: YESTERDAY YOU SAID TOMORROW 73
   REMOVE TEMPTATIONS 79
      Learn to Say No 81

    Plan of Action 82
  Create the Right Environment 85
  Strategies to Help You Overcome Procrastination 86
    Find a Mentor 86
    Don't Overcomplicate Anything 87
    Break Your Work into Small Steps 88

CHAPTER 6: INCREASE YOUR SELF-CONFIDENCE 93
  How to Build Your Self-Confidence 95
    Use Affirmations 97
    Imagine What You Want to Become 100
    Help Someone Else 103
    Do One Thing that Scares You Every Day 105
    Set Yourself Up to Win 106
    When You are Struggling, Look at What You Have Already Achieved 107

CHAPTER 7: BUILD WILLPOWER 111
  Two Main Parts of Building Willpower 111
    Motivating Yourself 114
    Recording Your Progress 117
  You Will Feel Drained 121
  You Must Be Willing to Fail 124

CHAPTER 8: CONTROL YOUR MIND 125
  Maintaining Focus 127
    Start Your Morning with a Routine 127
    Focus on Good Fats in Your Food 128
    Keep an Hour by Hour Planner 128
    Get Enough Sleep 129
  Meditation 130

CHAPTER 9: CHANGE YOUR HABITS 133

CONCLUSION 137

REFERENCES 140

Introduction

How many times have you told yourself, "I will worry about it tomorrow" or "I can't go to the gym today. I just don't have the energy"? Have you ever had two weeks to finish a project, but you've been chilling for 12 days, and on the thirteenth day, you started to freak out that you don't have enough time to do the work properly? How many times have you told yourself, "If only I had better self-discipline, I wouldn't procrastinate so much"?

Life puts obstacles and difficulties in your way to success, and to stand above them, you must work with determination and confidence. This, of course, requires self-discipline. The mastery of this skill leads to self-confidence and self-esteem, resulting in happiness and satisfaction with your work and life. On the other hand, the lack of self-discipline may lead to failure, destruction, well-being or relationship problems, health problems, etc.

For many people, self-discipline represents a genuine and allusive element that often slips through their fingertips. Speaking not only about bigger tasks you want to complete, achieving your goals, and reaching your dreams, but also little things like running errands need to be mastered and completed, so you're on the point with your to-do list and are able to set up a clear timing. These daily things just must be done, and we have to realize they might eat up hours of our day. We need to count on them and plan them accordingly. There is a plenitude of fields in our daily life where many of us want to do better.

According to the millions of people making the New Year's resolutions every year, this fact is especially obvious. All those resolutions usually involve losing weight, creating a healthier lifestyle, saving more money, improving the financial status and relationships, and eliminating bad habits (i.e., smoking, drinking, etc.).

However, less than 10% of these resolutions are observed. The main reason why it's like that is people set either too many or too unrealistic goals to achieve. They may be victims of the so-called "false hope syndrome," which is defined as a person's unrealistic expectations about the possible speed, amount, ease, and consequences of changing their behavior.

For many people, it requires a radical change in their attitude. It may take a medical diagnosis to make you give up alcohol, and it may require pregnancy to give up smoking. To transform your common behavior, you first have to change your thinking.

This book is all about learning tips and strategies to help you strengthen your self-discipline so you can focus on your tasks and become successful.

My aim in this book is to give you the tools you need to become mentally tough and master your self-discipline. It won't be the easiest journey that you take in your life, but it is one of the most rewarding and helpful journeys that will keep you going. It will strengthen your confidence, which will make you believe in yourself. You will learn what you are truly capable of accomplishing, which money cannot buy. Your time is now. Maybe you have been thinking about improving your self-discipline for years. Now you're in the right place to take control of your life. Stop allowing your inner critic and other negative thoughts to take over. It is time to truly know what you are capable of and reach for the stars.

Part 1: Theory

"Self-discipline is often disguised as short-term pain, which often leads to long-term gains. The mistake many of us make is the need and want for short-term gains (immediate gratification), which often leads to long-term pain."

— Charles F. Glassman

Chapter 1: Conquer Your Mind, Conquer the World

You are here because you want to improve your life. You might want to focus more on the tasks you need to complete at work. You might feel that your life needs more of a balance between work, time with your family, friends, and time for yourself. You might also be here because you want to improve your mindset by focusing on your self-discipline. No matter why you choose this book, the first step to mastering your self-discipline is understanding and developing it. The first step in this process is to conquer your mind, allowing you to conquer your world. When I talk about conquering your world, I mean the world around you—the parts of the world you can control. The pieces of this include your mind, emotions, and actions. You can't control what other people do, say, or think. However, you can control how you react to other people's attitudes and actions.

Understanding Self-Discipline

People often struggle with self-discipline because they must step out of their comfort zone to improve themselves. It is a working progress that you will focus on every day of your life. You won't be perfect at it every day, but you will always do your best, and this is exactly what you need to do. It is always important to take the success along with the failures as this shows your progress.

What Is Self-Discipline

"Self-discipline is the magic power that makes you virtually unstoppable."

- Anonymous

Self-discipline is controlling your own thoughts, emotions, actions, and desires through self-improvement methods. The goal is that you will focus on developing your self-discipline by trying to better yourself every day. Learning self-discipline is not easy, but you will quickly notice the benefits and strive to better yourself in order to keep those benefits in your life.

Many people see self-discipline as an uneasy and difficult road to follow. As someone who has worked on developing self-discipline for years, I will admit it is not easy. There are days when you find yourself struggling more than most to stay in your disciplined mindset. However, once you gain willpower, you will find a strategy that works for you. You will find yourself practicing self-discipline throughout your day. It will become a natural part of your routine.

Self-discipline is not denying yourself life's pleasures. It is not making sure you always walk in a straight line along your life's path. There are always bumps, curves, and even some potholes that you need to navigate, which might take you a bit off course. Self-discipline is a pleasant experience that you will find achievable. You will start to notice some of the benefits within days of working on your self-discipline, which will keep you more focused. In many ways, self-discipline is part of the puzzle of your life. Sometimes you lose the pieces, and you need to look for them. Sometimes they are right in front of your face, and other times it seems they fall from the sky and directly into place.

Self-discipline is one of the most important life skills for people to develop. Many people, especially those who have mastered self-discipline, compare it to a superpower because it allows you to remain mindful of your actions, thoughts, and emotions.

Mindfulness is when you are aware of everything going on in your environment — especially yourself. You notice if you ate enough, you know when you start to feel overwhelmed, when your thoughts are negative, or when you are tired and need to rest.

> Mindfulness and self-discipline go together. You cannot have one without the other.

This is because the opposite of mindfulness is mindlessness, which is when you are not aware of your environment, thoughts, emotions, and actions. Take a moment to think about driving your regular route to work, the grocery store, or your friend's house. You are used to the scenery and know exactly where you are going, so you let your mind wander. When you park your vehicle, you ask yourself how you got there because you don't remember part of the route. This is an example of becoming mindless. If you are mindful, you remember everything about your drive.

Developing Your Self-Discipline

The most critical part of reaching your goals is developing your self-discipline. The struggle people tend to have is the resistance they feel, pulling them away from their self-discipline. For example, you started a new diet last week and are struggling to stay away from the food you love but can't have. Even though you threw away all the food in your home that you aren't allowed to eat on a diet, you continue to see the food everywhere. Potato chips, which are your favorite snacks, are not acceptable on this diet. You have been craving potato chips for several days and are not sure how much longer you can stay away from your favorite snack. Your mind keeps telling you, "Just a few won't hurt you; buy a small bag and go for a long walk in the morning." After a few more days, you decide to have a cheat day and feed your cravings. You tell yourself, "It will be better tomorrow. Besides, I have had a tough week, and everyone deserves a cheat day now and then."

The belief in cheat days leads people to lose their self-discipline when they start a diet. It is the thoughts you have that tell you, "It is okay to have a few cookies, as long as you don't do it every day," that keep you from strengthening your self-discipline.

There are dozens of ways you can develop your self-discipline. You don't have to follow the path that other people have taken — you can develop your own plan and what works for your lifestyle and personality. In fact, you are more likely to succeed on your self-discipline journey if you develop your own path based on what you need.

Before I take you further into your self-development journey, you need to know these tips that will help you master your self-discipline.

1. **Set clear goals.** One of the biggest reasons people struggle with self-discipline is because they do not establish clear goals. They have an idea of the goal they want to reach, but they don't think about the process of this goal. They don't form steps that will help them remain focused on their goals.
2. **Create a backup plan.** A backup plan will help you through a difficult time or a moment when you find a fault in your original plan. Backup plans don't mean that you must stop focusing on your original plan. They simply mean that you will help yourself through the bumps in your path.
3. **Know your weaknesses.** Your weaknesses are nothing to be ashamed of as everyone has weaknesses, just like everyone has strengths. The key is to understand your

weaknesses, as this will guide you to know what direction you need to take on the path to reach your self-discipline. The only way you will overcome your weakness is by admitting you have them.

4. **Keep your new habits simple.** Trying to follow a new habit can be a daunting task because it is hard to break your old habits. One way to keep yourself from feeling intimidated is to create simple new habits. For example, if you want to start working out for an hour every day to lose weight and get in shape, you will begin by exercising 15 minutes a day. Once you become more motivated to exercise, add 5 to 10 minutes to your time. Slowly increase your time until you are exercising for an hour a day.

5. **Believe you have willpower.** When you believe you have willpower, you know you can achieve your goals. You will continue to build your motivation to succeed, which will increase your self-esteem and self-image. This will help you become a more positive person and continue to keep you motivated, even when you hit the bumps in the road.

6. **Learn from your mistakes.** You will stumble from time to time, no matter how strong your self-discipline becomes. You can establish the best steps to reach your goals and still find yourself struggling. This happens to everyone, and it is important not to let it get you down.

Acknowledge what happened and continue to move forward. When you start letting yourself feel angry or guilty, you will continue to struggle and slow down your progress. You can't succeed without failure.

7. **Reward yourself.** One of the important steps in establishing your goals is making sure you set rewards for yourself. You want to treat yourself in a way that will keep you motivated to continue. For example, you might watch an episode of your favorite show on Netflix, go to the movies with a friend, or go out to eat.

Self-Confidence Vs. Self-Esteem

As an entrepreneur, Roger has recently learned he needs to work on self-improvement by taking control of his self-discipline. A couple of months ago, Roger started his own writing business, where he works for several clients as a writer and editor. Recently, Roger started to notice that he is not following his schedule, he is easily distracted, and he doesn't always have the willpower to sit at his desk and work. Roger knows that he doesn't lack the motivation for his work or lost interest in his job. He enjoys writing and has put in a lot of work over the last few years to establish his business.

Roger first realized his struggles getting into his schedule within his first week of working from home. At this time, Roger contributed his struggles to years of stress working two jobs. Not only did Roger focus on developing his business, but he also worked full-time as a journalist. His job often caused him to work more than 40 hours a week and odd hours to cover evening and weekend events. It caused him to lack a schedule with both jobs.

Furthermore, Roger worked close to 100 hours a week for over six months. These factors made Roger think he was dealing with the aftereffects of eliminating a huge amount of stress from his shoulders. He talked to His friends about his struggles, and they agreed that in a couple of weeks, Roger would start to focus more on his schedule and continue to build his business. But, almost two months later, Roger is still struggling.

Roger has an idea of what self-discipline is but doesn't have a clear idea of effectively reaching self-discipline. He has never focused on improving his self-discipline and is unsure of the steps he will need to take. Roger starts to research self-discipline and incorporate its strategies into his life to have more motivation to follow his schedule and complete his tasks. The first point Roger learns is that he is already improving because he understands that he needs to work on his self-discipline. Roger is already improving because he acknowledges his weaknesses and focuses on establishing good self-discipline strategies to continue to grow his business and general self-improvement.

One of the first factors Roger realized about himself was his low self-confidence. He didn't realize all the negative thoughts he had throughout the day. He didn't notice how often he questioned his abilities as a writer and editor. Even though his clients loved his work, he continued to believe that his talent could vanish in an instant. He felt that his clients would find someone better, and his business would fail. Roger realized that he needed to change his mindset to gain a stronghold of his self-discipline.

One day at a time, Roger started building his plan to control his emotions and thoughts. He used strategies to become more mindful and started reflecting on his day by journaling for 15 minutes before going to bed. In the morning, he got up a half-hour early and started to meditate before getting ready for the day. He started to eat healthier, focusing on smaller meals and eating more often. Roger started snacking on healthy foods over cookies, chips, and candy. He gave up soda, started drinking more water, and got at least 7 hours of sleep every night. Over time, Roger started to feel better emotionally, mentally, and physically.

Like Roger, you don't think about self-discipline because you become comfortable with your daily routine and habits. They become a part of your life, and that is just the way it is. Another reason you don't spend a lot of thought on self-discipline is because of your low self-confidence.

It is important to understand the difference between self-confidence and self-esteem. You can have high self-esteem and still have low self-confidence. Your self-esteem is how you feel about yourself overall. You focus on the positive experiences that have happened throughout your life, giving you a positive outlook. Self-confidence is how you feel about your abilities and talents. You might think that your artwork or writing is never good enough or that you aren't good at math. However, you will feel that you are strong in other areas, such as interior decorating. Self-confidence can change from one situation to the next.

When you start observing yourself in the mission to increase your self-discipline, you will notice that you have high self-confidence where your self-discipline is strong. When your self-discipline is weak, your self-confidence is also weak. Your self-discipline follows how confident you feel about certain situations. To help you understand, think about a skill you feel you aren't good at. How motivated are you when it comes to focusing on that skill? For example, if you feel you aren't a good artist, you won't spend a lot of time drawing or painting. But, if your confidence is high as an artist, you are often motivated to work on your projects. If you need to, take some time to write down skills you are confident about and skills where your self-confidence is low. Then, take a moment to think about how motivated you are to focus on these skills. Write down how you feel about the skills and think of ways to start to build your self-confidence, thus building your self-discipline in these skills.

> Self-discipline is a skill, which is something that you learn over time. Developing your self-discipline takes time, patience, and commitment.

You will find yourself feeling like you can't build your self-discipline, and you will have days when you are strong in this area of your life. Everything you feel as you work towards strengthening your self-discipline is normal. In the moments where you start to question yourself, take a moment to think about what you have accomplished. Above all, you always need to remember that you are on the right path and do a great job. You are not alone in this struggle. Always be proud of your improvements.

Chapter 2: Mindset

The key to improving your self-discipline is your mindset. This is something that I had to learn by myself, which is something I want to make easier for you. I felt alone as I knew I needed to change how I felt about myself, which made my journey even harder. Once I realized that I wasn't alone, that there were thousands of other people trying to change their mindset, I started to grow a little by little each day.

I didn't receive a lot of support as a child. I remember coming home to my parents laughing at a story I had written when I was 12 years old. As a child, writing was a way to escape the struggles I faced daily. When my parents found my notebook and made fun of everything, I lost all confidence in my ability as a growing writer. I stopped writing for many years and started to keep to myself more. I couldn't find a different way to work through my thoughts and emotions, so they continued to pile up inside me. Eventually, they became unbearable. However, I continued to remain quiet because I didn't want to cause a scene. I didn't want people to start thinking I was crazy or couldn't control myself.

In my third year of college, I was about to flunk out when a professor reached out to me. He told me what a gift I had for writing and how much he enjoyed reading my papers. I didn't know what to say other than "thank you," so I just stood there awkwardly. I left his classroom, thinking that he would change his mind the next time. After all, I had no talent for writing.

He never changed his mind. In fact, more professors started to talk to me about my papers and told me I should think about taking technical and creative writing courses to expand my writing. Finally, I opened up to one of my professors and told him that I wouldn't work on my writing because it really wasn't that good, and eventually, he would believe it too. I will never forget how his mouth dropped and how quickly he shook his head. He then told me, "No, you just don't realize how good you are yet. Come to my office tomorrow after class as I want to show you something."

The next day I followed him back to his office. He had me sit beside him on his couch and told me that I was going to learn how to meditate. He told me about his childhood struggles and how meditation was his first step in changing his mindset. For three days every week, I went to his office, and we spent 10 minutes meditating.

After a couple of weeks, he gave me an inspirational book of quotes. He told me to read one quote every time I noticed a negative thought or feeling. He also gave me a journal and told me to start writing about my day before I went to bed every night. I could write about how I felt during certain situations and how I changed my negative thoughts into positive thoughts.

As the weeks went by, I gradually started to focus more on positivity. I found myself reading an inspirational quote and listening to a motivational video on YouTube every morning. When I struggled during the day, I would take out my book of quotes and read one.

A decade later, I now believe I am a talented writer. Of course, I still have my days where my mindset is a bit weaker. These days, I focus more on the strategies I have learned throughout these last few years to gain more confidence and refocus my mindset.

I didn't realize that changing our mindset is a choice until I noticed my own teenage son struggling with his mindset after dealing with bullying in school. It wasn't that I couldn't change my mindset as a teenager or without the help of my professor. It was that I didn't truly understand and didn't believe I could. It was my choice to continue focusing on the negativity in my life. This is now something that I am trying to teach my teenager — you need to say yes and know what you really want.

Fixed and Growth Mindset

As you can see from my story, changing your mindset will not happen overnight. It is a process that you will spend years on. In fact, you will focus on growing your mindset for the rest of your life. This doesn't mean every day will be one struggle after another, where you will need to take time for yourself and focus on the positives over the negatives. You will have days when you feel choosing your positive mindset over the negative is natural and days when you need to work at it a little more.

It Is Always Your Choice

After years of focusing on developing a more positive and calmer mindset, I still have days where I need to choose to spend more time on the positives than the negatives. There are days when I lack energy and feel that lying in bed thinking about my bad day is the best option. However, I know that always focusing on growing and fixing my mindset is completely up to me. So, what do I do? I accept my bad day and focus on the happy moments. I take my moment to sit in the dark and reflect on the negative parts of my day. Then, I start to focus on the positives. I start at the beginning and think about how my family is healthy and happy. I focus on my job and how much I enjoy what I do. I think about all the progress I have made with my mindset over the last few years. Slowly, my mindset begins to change. I start to feel that this day is one day. It doesn't define who I am.

It is easy to get 'down in the dumps' when you are having a bad day. There are days when climbing out of the dumps is easier and some days when it is harder. There are days when opening your inspirational book of quotes will not help like it normally does, but will make you feel worse. In these moments, you need to continue to focus on your strategies to grow your mindset. The key to remember in these moments is how you respond to your mindset is *your choice*. Ask yourself, "Am I going to sit here and feel bad for myself, or am I going to pick myself up, dust myself off, and start fresh?" Remember, you can start fresh at any moment throughout your day.

Fixed Mindset

A fixed mindset is one of the two main types of mindsets people have. A fixed mindset is when you don't focus on growing your mindset through strategies. When you have a fixed mindset, you believe your abilities are fixed within you and cannot change. This means that you won't improve your mindset because you don't believe it is possible.

A fixed mindset doesn't mean you have low self-confidence or self-esteem. You value your worth, and you know what you can achieve, but you don't believe you can go beyond what you believe is set for you.

A fixed mindset means that you believe your talent is what will bring you success. You won't reach success by working hard or putting more effort into your career. For example, you tell yourself that you are good or something or you're not. You believe that even if you try to accomplish a task that you aren't good at, you will fail. Therefore, you don't believe in wasting your time trying to achieve a new task. Instead, you continue to focus on what you are good at. Another example of a fixed mindset is refusing to learn anything new because you already know everything you need to know.

You might have developed your fixed mindset because of the way you were raised, or you were told that you couldn't improve. For example, you decided to pick up the flute for a band in school. You practiced often and found yourself as one of the top flute players. While you continued to practice, your parents and band instructor started to tell you that you couldn't get any better as a flute player. You were already the first chair and took the lead in programs. Because of this, you started to feel stuck and didn't think there was another goal for you as a flute player. Therefore, you developed a fixed mindset when it came to playing the flute.

Growth Mindset

A growth mindset is the opposite of a fixed mindset. If you have a growth mindset, you believe that you can continue to learn and improve over time. In fact, you believe that you can always improve your mindset if you work on it. There is always time to learn something new and give yourself better opportunities.

If you have a fixed mindset, it is possible to develop a growth mindset. Carol Dweck, Professor of Psychology at Stanford University, wrote a book titled *Mindset: The New Psychology of Success*, where she talks about growth and fixed mindsets in depth. Through her research, Dweck described the fixed and growth mindset. Since then, several psychologists and other researchers have worked on strategies to transform your fixed mindset into a growth mindset.

- **See challenges as opportunities.** You face challenges every day. You might have to find the answer to a difficult question, such as whether you should take a new job or accomplish a new task at work. If you see challenges as a roadblock, it is time to view them as an opportunity for growth. Take time to think about how you can grow with the challenge and visualize yourself overcoming this challenge.

- **Never stop learning.** You might not be in school anymore, but this doesn't mean you stop learning. You can continue to learn every day by reading and learning new tasks. Learning will help you understand that your brain is constantly learning new information, which helps it grow.
- **Needing to improve does not mean you are a failure.** Needing to improve in any area of your life doesn't mean you are failing. It means that you still have room for growth and to become your best self.
- **Don't be afraid of failure.** Failure doesn't mean that you can't do something. It means that you need to try again. Learn from your mistakes and move on. Think of failure as an opportunity to establish more strengths in your life.
- **Learn well, not fast.** There is a difference between learning something well and learning it quickly. Even if you feel you need to learn your new task quickly, it is more important that you understand the steps of your task. You want to perform your work well and not quickly.

To Learn or Not to Learn?

Part of your self-discipline mastery is to achieve the mindset that learning is living. You want to make learning a priority, as this will open your mind to all areas of your life. It will give you more motivation to continue building your self-discipline. Learning also helps you manage your self-discipline because you become more aware of your actions and emotions.

Most people think they can only learn in school. They believe that learning comes from the classroom. This isn't true. In fact, you are learning right and probably not sitting in a classroom as you are reading this book.

To make learning a priority in your life, you need to keep your eyes and ears open. You need to focus when you are learning and note it within your mind. The more interested you are in what you are learning, the more you will remember it. If you are learning something new by reading a book and moving on to another activity without giving what you have learned another thought, you will not remember it.

Understand the World

You need to look around your environment. You need to understand what is going on. For example, if you walk down the street and see someone looking like a homeless on the street corner with a sign. As you walk closer, you see the sign that reads, "Anything will help." The sign tugs at your heartstrings as you begin to realize there are holes in the person's shoes. You see, their hair is a mess, and they are not clean. You then notice all the cars driving by. Some people stare at the person, while others act like they don't notice anyone is standing there.

You walk up to the person and give them what little cash you have in your pocket. They tell you, "Thank you so much. God bless you." You are about to walk away, but then stop and think you want to know more. You want to know why the person is in this situation. You want to know if they know of any resources around the area. You want to know whatever information they can give you because you want to help this person and every homeless person in your area. While you don't live in a large city, you know there are several resources for the homeless in your city, and all of them struggle to help everyone on the streets. This tells you that there is a lack of help for the homeless in your area. You turn around and ask if the person will talk to you for a bit over a meal. They agree, and you head to the local restaurant.

As you are about to walk in, you notice that the person who has recently introduced themselves to you as Sam set their cart directly in front of the window. They then ask you, "Would you mind if we sit right there so I can watch my stuff. It's all I have." You agree as you open the door.

When you have a mission to help the homeless, one of the best ways to learn how to get into the nonprofit world to help them is by talking to people. You want to talk to the homeless people in your area and any other nonprofits aiming to help the homeless. Talk to as many people and organizations as you can to get a clear and thorough understanding. You might find that while there are plenty of places homeless people can get food and clothing, there aren't enough places in the area that can offer them a place to sleep. Therefore, you learn that what your community needs is a nonprofit that will help with this resource. You might discover that you not only have a place that offers a few beds, but you work with churches in the area to create more space for them to sleep, especially when the nights are cold.

Teach Other People About Your World

Another part of learning is to teach other people about your world. You want to take action for what you have learned, as this will further your understanding. At the same time, you need to realize there are different ways to understand the concept. For instance, people will understand homelessness differently from you. Some people may have found themselves homeless for a while, and this gives them a different view. Other people may have helped someone only to find out that they were scamming for money and now have a sour point of view about homeless people.

You need to become open to your experiences and have patience when you are talking to other people. At the same time, you also need to understand their experiences and what they feel about the situation you are discussing. For example, if a person brushes you off because they don't believe homelessness is a problem in the community, you can show them statistics instead of talking about your experience.

Treat Learning as an Inspiration

There are two ways that you can learn. You can learn on autopilot, or you can become interested in what you are learning. When you become interested, you will feel inspired. You will want to learn as much as possible and help other people understand what you have learned. Treating learning as an inspiration will allow you to focus on the quality throughout the project.

Learning Helps Your Mindset Grow

You can't continue to grow your mindset without learning. You need to focus on your task, your environment, and listen to other people in order to have a growth mindset. This is because, with a growth mindset, you focus on progress and look for opportunities to help expand your knowledge and abilities. For example, Roger soon started to learn about the opportunities writing had for him — opportunities he never thought of until he started his writing business and started to gain the self-confidence he needed to develop as a writer.

One of the factors Roger learned that he loved to focus on as a writer was helping other writers. He believed in his talent and started to open up to other writers about how he develops, the mindset he uses, and how he starts his writing process. Over time, Roger started to notice that other writers came to him for advice. This quickly became one of Roger's favorite tasks. He wanted to help other writers develop.

As Roger started researching what other job opportunities were available for him as a writer, he came across the opportunity to be a writing coach. Looking more into this job, he noted that it was what he enjoyed doing the most. He looked at the qualification for a certificate and decided to save little money from his paychecks to pay for the certification.

Roger established becoming a writing coach as a goal and developed the steps to ensure he would reach his goal within two years.

Chapter 3: Key to Success

Think back to when you were a child and how did you see the world. How you looked at the world and learned about everything around you. It depends on how far back you remember. For example, if you remember being a small child, you might remember the feeling when everything was new to you. Your mind was busy trying to learn everything that you come across every day. If you remember the age of 9, you probably only learned because of school. You didn't care to learn too much outside of school, at least for the most part. Instead, you loved to relax and spend more time doing the activities you enjoyed. As a teenager, your interest in learning subsided. It felt more like a job you had to do when you would rather sit at home and watch television or play video games.

At least if you are like Drake, you don't care to learn much as a teenager. Drake's mother, Amirah, didn't understand what had happened to her son's grades. He used to receive A's and B's. Sometimes his grades would drop down to a C, but he could bring them back up quickly. Since the age of 12, Amirah has noticed her son's grades are lower. He usually struggles to keep his grades at C's and has more D's. This quarter, he even has an F, which he has never received before. Amirah and her husband have worked with the school to make sure their son has everything he needs. They help him with his homework, at least when he brings it home.

Amirah has tried to talk to Drake countless times about his grades and what he needs. However, he always tells her that he doesn't know what is going on or the work isn't interesting. In the middle of the first quarter, Amirah realized she had to limit her son's screen time more because he would lie about any homework so he could play his games or watch television. She felt that making sure he had time to do any homework, even if it was only reading, would help. Unfortunately, Drake continues to struggle with his grades.

But, it's not just school that Drake doesn't have an interest in when it comes to learning. He would rather not do any type of learning. He loved going to museums and learning about different cultures and topics with his mom, but he didn't care to do any of these activities anymore. At one time, Amirah worried her son was depressed. However, the therapist informed her that Drake just isn't interested in learning like he used to be, which is normal for many kids. "Some children just stop caring about learning when they become preteens or teenagers. As long as you continue to focus on the value of education, Drake will come around. He still has goals of going to college, which is good. This is only a phase and nothing really to worry about. Do what you can to get him to keep his grades up and work on his homework. If you find himself struggling more, come back, and I will see if there is anything else I can do."

Not every child is like Drake. Many kids thrive on learning throughout their life. However, some children would rather start to focus on something else than what they are learning. One reason for this is that if they aren't interested in it, they don't want to learn it. Another reason children stop willing to learn at a certain age is they lack motivation. Some children stop learning because they don't understand the value of education. Sometimes the child's role model is the reason they don't want to learn anymore. They feel that if their parents don't focus on learning, why should they? Another reason is that they might feel the task is too hard. They might have anxiety or give up easily because they don't think they can complete the task.

No matter what the reason for your child's disinterest in learning, it is up to you to do what you can to help them through this process calmly and rationally. Realize that you can talk until you are blue in the face, and they might not take another step into learning. You can explain how important their grades are for college, but they might not want to go to college. In reality, it is difficult to get your child to learn when they don't care to do so. Sometimes taking away their phones or gaming privileges doesn't help as much as you thought it would.

Motivated to Learn

You don't have to be a preteen or teenager to become unmotivated to learn. Some students are in their third year of college and find themselves becoming less focused on learning. Some people struggle with learning once they graduate from college and become comfortable in their job. They don't feel that learning is a part of their lifestyle anymore. Whatever your age or reasoning for losing your motivation to learn, there are several strategies you can follow to change your habits and focus more on learning. After all, you won't reach your self-discipline mastery without learning every day.

- **Take the time to read every day.** You don't have to spend a lot of time reading, but it should be enjoyable. Don't force yourself to read a book that you aren't interested in. You can include reading as part of your daily routine. For example, get up half an hour earlier every morning and read. If your child struggles with learning, find a book that they will be interested in and include them in this process. It doesn't matter if your child focuses on reading a comic book. As long as they are reading, you are helping them increase their willingness to learn.

- **Focus on interests.** There will always be topics you are not interested in learning. Your child will always have subjects in school that they struggle with because 'math isn't their thing.' This is okay. It is a part of life. Of course, you don't want them to have bad grades but understand that this subject is harder for them because they aren't interested. Instead of focusing on what isn't interesting, you want to focus on what is. For example, if your child is interested in video games, encourage them to explore the ways video games are created.
- **Learn something new every day.** Take time every day to talk to your child about something new that you learned. Ask them to share something that they learned throughout the day. This can be anything they learned; it doesn't have to be a part of their school day. Encourage them to explore more about the world around them and show them that you will do the same.
- **Watch videos.** You're not limited anymore only to reading books like your parents and grandparent were. Use the digital age and explore the thousands of educative videos on the internet about any topic you can think of. If you're willing to incorporate more learning into your daily routine and you can't fit reading a book into your schedule, watch a video or listen to a podcast while you walk to work, the gym, or on a treadmill in the gym.

Grow Your Mental Toughness

What does it mean to grow your mental toughness? It means that you learn to resist and overcome your concerns, worries, doubts, and anything or anyone that keeps you from succeeding. Your mindset becomes tough as you realize no one can tell you what your self-worth is — you are the only person who knows your self-worth.

Mental toughness means that you need to consciously work on your growth mindset, but you also need to focus on this in steps. The first step is to master your mindset. This means you have to take in all the theories you have read through this book and apply them to your life. The next part will help you work through the steps to develop your mindset and mental toughness and achieve your self-discipline mastery.

Mental toughness does not mean that you are self-absorbed and don't notice what other people say about you. It doesn't mean that you are unemotional. Mental toughness doesn't mean that you don't appreciate people or that you are unkind. People who have mental toughness are very compassionate, understanding, and willing to help other people at a moment's notice. Mental toughness does not mean you are physically tough, as it has nothing to do with your physical strength. It focuses on your emotional and mental strength. While you want to have a positive mindset, mental toughness is not all about positive thinking. It is about being realistic and rational in your thinking. It is about maintaining a clear mind.

Mental toughness is a mindset that leads you to success because you won't let failure or roadblocks stop you. You are self-confident in your abilities, and you know your self-worth. Mental toughness is the mind of an entrepreneur — someone who understands that people will say hurtful statements about them or their company and understands that this does not define their business. What defines their business is their actions, the actions of their employees, and how they handle criticism.

Mental toughness is a skill that will help you in all areas of your life. For example, Roger finds himself quickly losing self-confidence as he deals with tough editors and clients who are harsh when it comes to the work Roger gives them. He tries to tell himself that revisions are part of the job for a ghostwriter. He understands that some clients don't give him enough information for the outline but have a very specific idea about what they want. However, this doesn't keep Roger from feeling a little disappointed when he is given a revision.

While Roger is talking to one of his co-workers, they tell him that he needs to develop a mentally tough attitude toward the ghostwriting business. As Roger continues to develop this attitude, he finds himself showing more leadership and confidence in other areas of his life, such as volunteering for a local nonprofit or coaching soccer. He finds himself becoming more driven to learn and spending less time in front of the television.

Core Distinctions of Mental Toughness

- **Preparation.** A mentally tough individual is prepared for anything that could happen. You develop a plan of action for your goals and often a backup plan.
- **Winning mindset.** Your winning mindset is the attitude you have, whether you win or lose in a game or find yourself accomplishing or failing at a task. This mindset is the belief that you will succeed. It is a mindset that is solid and doesn't waver.
- **Focus.** You find yourself peaking with your best performance, and don't allow yourself to become distracted. You keep your mind clear, and many people state that you get "into the zone" when working on a task.
- **Stress management.** You can handle stress well. Even when your job becomes stressful, you remain focused, and you don't allow stress to affect you in your job or

professional life. You understand that part of succeeding is stress, and you need to experience this part of the job to understand what you can truly accomplish.

Mental toughness is the part of your mindset that you will develop constantly. Even when you feel like you have reached your maximum toughness, you will continue to work on its development as you are always working on your mindset.

Benefits of Mental Toughness

Mental toughness is a newer phenomenon globally, but it is quickly becoming popular because of its benefits.

- You will focus more on helpful advice and tune out advice that won't help you along your journey.
- You will feel more motivated to continue your journey, even when you run into negativity, whether this is a negative review of your business or people who don't support you.
- You will handle negative reviews in a more rational way. You will look at what the reviewer says and at the source of the review. You will note if the reviewer is logical with their judgment or not. If they are not, you will find yourself moving on from the situation. If they are, you will take their review as advice and incorporate it into your business or another area of your life.

- You gain the courage to face your fears through mental toughness. You become more comfortable with stepping outside of your comfort zone. You understand that feeling uncomfortable leads you to success.
- You are more in control of your emotions through mental toughness. You think rationally about the situation in front of you and don't make decisions based on your emotions.
- You bounce back from failure quickly. You see failure as a learning opportunity and are ready to persevere and reach the next stage in your life.

One of the best benefits of mental toughness is that you don't let people control your career or life. You develop a tough mind that allows you to stay on the right track to reach success. Even if your friends or family members try to push you off track, you will find yourself overcoming their push and pull to focus on what is best for you. You will learn to let go of the people who don't support you and focus on those who do.

An example of the growth of mental toughness and how it affects you in your personal and professional life comes from a young woman named Amirah. She grew up in a home that many people would call average. She felt unappreciated by her parents. She never felt truly loved by them because they pushed her to the side. They focused more on what they wanted than on what she needed. It didn't matter if she brought good or bad grades home from school. Her parents didn't respond in any way. There were times she had to forge her mother's signature on school papers because her parents weren't home to sign the papers or refused to do it, as it was a waste of their time.

With the help of her high school guidance counselor and teachers, Amirah applied for college, received financial aid, and started her freshman year hours away from her parents. Amirah decided that at the start of her college years, she would focus on herself. She didn't need her parents for anything. She would make new friends and establish a new family.

Amirah didn't understand what mental toughness was until she took a general psychology course. At that moment, Amirah realized that she had to work on developing her self-confidence and her mental toughness. She knew how helpful this would become when she became a business owner in the future. Mental toughness would help Amirah reach her goals, just like self-confidence and self-discipline.

Through a series of strategies, Amirah focused on gaining control of her emotions. She started focusing on the comments from her professors about her papers as ways to improve her abilities. She took any type of criticism to develop her mindset. Amirah noticed which friends supported her and who wanted her to party with them. Because partying wouldn't help her mindset, Amirah stopped hanging out with her party friends and focused on her more educated friends.

At her college graduation, Amirah thought about the person she was when she entered college. She remembered being a scared young girl who didn't believe she would finish college. She thought she would drop out because it would become too hard. Now, she is valedictorian and giving her speech in front of thousands of people about mental toughness and how it helps on the road to success. Amirah is now confident that she will one day run a successful business.

Once you reach a stage of mental toughness, you are more satisfied with your life. You feel proud of yourself and what you have accomplished. You understand that failure will happen, but this doesn't mean you can't continue to develop your skills. You don't have to let failure take you off your path. Instead, you will fall forward, pick yourself up, dust yourself off, and try again. You will continue to try until you succeed because your mindset tells you that failure doesn't mean giving up. It means that you are trying, and you will become successful as you continue to work on it.

Part 2: Practice

"We can be truly successful only at something we're willing to fail at."

– Mark Manson

Chapter 4: Think Big, Start Small

You have a list of tasks you want to accomplish. However, it seems that your list of goals continues to grow without you marking any of them off. You start to wonder if you will ever reach some of the goals you set for yourself. As you think about some of your goals, you realize how big they are, but you know you can achieve them—you are not always sure how, but you know it is possible.

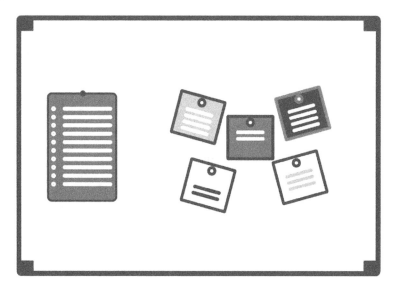

One of the biggest practices when maintaining self-discipline is to create smaller steps for your goals. It doesn't matter how small you think your goal is. You always want to break it down into smaller steps. Think of your goal as the top of your stairs, and each step you take is reaching one of the smaller goals that will lead you to achieve your main goal.

You don't want to make the mistake of setting your goal and finding yourself struggling to reach it because you didn't understand how to get started, what to do, or that the goal is too big for you. When you find yourself struggling with your goals, you are more likely to believe that you can't reach them. This will affect you psychologically and damage some of the self-discipline you have built.

Golden Goal Setting Rules

To help you get into the mindset of developing smaller goals within a larger goal, it is important to understand the golden rules for setting goals.

Write Down Your Goals

How often have you written down your goals compared to keeping them locked away in your mind? You probably discuss your goals with family, friends, co-workers, and other people in your life, but have you ever sat down and written out your goals? If not, physically writing out your goals can help make your goal real to you. While you might feel you want to achieve your goal when you think about it, you have thousands of thoughts going through your mind a day. You might have an idea of how to reach your goal, but how much work do you put toward your goal every day? Have you ever forgotten about any goals you wanted to accomplish or pushed them to the side because you didn't feel they were important enough? Were you too busy to focus on them? If so, the real reason you might have forgotten or pushed them away is that you didn't write them down.

When you write your goals down on paper, you want to use words like "will" instead of "might." You want to make the goal as concrete as possible. For example, instead of writing, "I would like to exercise for 30 minutes each day," you write, "I will exercise for 30 minutes every morning."

When you write down your goals, you want to frame them positively. You will write the way you think about your goal, so if you aren't completely sure you will reach your goal, this will come out in your writing. Then, when you look at your written goals, you won't feel as confident about achieving them, especially if you doubt your goals. For example, if you write, "I will try to stick to my diet and say goodbye to all the yummy food," it isn't a motivational goal. You can feel negatively about this goal because it will make you feel that you are saying goodbye to your favorite foods and forcing yourself on this diet. You want to word the goal in a way that highlights your new diet positively. For example, you write, "I will stick to my diet to improve my overall health."

Use the SMART Rule

You can create goals or SMART goals. SMART stands for the five characteristics that every goal should be expressed as:

- *Specific*. Specific goals are well-defined and clear. You know exactly what you want and what steps you will take to reach your goal.
- *Measurable*. You want to include a plan to measure the progress of your goal. For example, you will have dates that give you a timeline of your goal. If you want to exercise for 30 minutes every morning, you will start exercising for 10 minutes every morning for two weeks. You will then increase your time by 5 minutes once a week until you reach 30 minutes.
- *Attainable*. Always know that you can achieve the goals you set. Of course, they can seem overwhelming at first, but your confidence will make you believe you can reach your goals. At the same time, you have to ensure that you work hard to achieve your goals. If you set goals that are too easy, you won't feel accomplished or grow out of your comfort zone.
- *Relevant*. Make sure your goals are relevant to the direction you want to take in your life. This will help you stay focused on your life's path and reach where you see yourself in three or five years.
- *Time-Bound*. Always make sure your goals have a deadline. The deadline might be in a month or three years. It all depends on the goal and its steps.

Your Goals Need to Keep You Motivated

If you set goals that don't motivate you to work on them, your goal setting won't work. A goal is something you want to achieve in your life. You need to ensure that your goals are important to you and direct you where you want to go in life. If you don't imagine the outcome of your goals or have little interest in them, you need to look at why. Are you thinking about your goal the right way? Are your goals something that you want to achieve in your life? Is your goal a priority?

> You need to have the "I must accomplish this goal" attitude to maximize the likelihood of achieving your goals. Not having a can-do-must-do attitude will make it very hard for you to reach and may leave you frustrated and disappointed in yourself.

Creating an Action Plan

Creating an action plan for each goal will help you follow through with them. You will remain excited, and each step you accomplish will give you more motivation to achieve your goal. It's not easy to look at a goal and then think about your action plan. To help you get more comfortable with this process, here are some tips for incorporating as you create your plan.

1. Make sure your goals are clear, and you know exactly what you want. Think about how you will describe your goal. Ensure that your goal is relevant to your life plans and is attainable.
2. Create the steps to reach your goal by going backward. For example, if you want to eliminate your debt within a year, you will look at how much you need to pay off every month, every three months, and during the sixth month period. Having an amount for each of these milestones will help you keep better track of the steps of your goal. Make sure you include a timeframe for each step.
3. Take each step one by one and focus on it. You need to determine what actions are required for you to reach your goal. For example, you will create a budget and notice

where you can save money or what money you can put toward your debt every month.

4. Ask yourself what reward you want to give yourself once you achieve each step and reach your goal. This reward needs to be something that will keep you motivated and something you don't give yourself regularly.

5. Create a daily plan. Ask yourself what you can do every day to make sure you reach your milestones and goals? For example, if you purchase lunch at work every day, how much money will you save if you pack a lunch from home? Will meal planning help you stick to the schedule? What other daily habits do you have that can help you save money or put it toward your debt?

6. It is common to feel like you have a chaotic paper full of goals and scribbles when you are done creating your plan. If you need to re-write your plan, you should do so. You want your plan to look clear and easy to follow, as this will keep you motivated.

7. Make sure that you remain consistent in your daily schedule. This will help you achieve your milestones. Follow through with the tasks you give yourself, and remember to stay away from your rewards until you complete a step.

The biggest key to reaching your goals is to focus on one milestone at a time. Even when you look at your whole goal on the sheet, you want to keep your mind focused on the milestone you are working on at that moment. This will help keep you focused, and you won't feel so overwhelmed by your goal.

When Roger wrote his action plan to help him follow a schedule, he decided to observe his natural behavior for a week and note anything that helped him follow through with his schedule and anything that kept him away from his schedule. The helpful behavior and actions that Roger wrote down included:

- Getting up by 7:00 A.M. and getting dressed.
- Having a healthy breakfast.
- Sitting at my desk by 8:00 A.M.
- Switching my phone to silent and keeping it in another room.
- Keeping the television in my office area/bedroom off.
- Taking a 10-minute break to walk around the apartment every hour, but not turning on the television or sitting down.
- Taking a one-hour lunch break where I leave my work and focus on a relaxing activity.

- Stop working at 6:00 P.M. and relaxing or focusing on other activities the rest of the night instead of continuing to work late or going back to work after an hour.

The behaviors and actions Roger noticed that didn't help him stick to his schedule included:

- Staying up late and allowing myself to sleep in.
- Staying up too late and napping during the day.
- Eating a heavy and unhealthy breakfast.
- Not getting ready for the day, such as starting work while still wearing pajamas.
- Keeping my phone next to me.
- Keeping the silent mode off.
- Having non-work tabs open online.
- Turning on the television or watching a YouTube video when I am on a break.
- Not leaving my desk during my break.
- Working from the time I get up until I go to bed. This decreases my willpower to work the next day.
- Snacking often.
- Taking more than my needed breaks.
- Not standing up to the point when I feel the need to move.
- Telling myself that "I can work on it later in the day. I have time."

Once Roger had a clear understanding of what behaviors and actions helped him and which ones didn't, he started to create his plan. His goal became "I will follow my work schedule of starting at 8:00 A.M. and working until 6:00 P.M. with one 10-minute break every hour and a one-hour lunch break."

Roger then started to write out the steps of his goal. He gave himself a month to accomplish the goal and felt this was an adequate amount of time. The steps Roger included to help him make his goal were:

1. Start going to bed at 11:00 P.M and set the alarm to get up at 7:00 A.M
2. Get up and get ready for the day, just as I would when working outside of my home.
3. Have a healthy breakfast, such as fruit and eggs with a slice of bacon or a sausage patty.
4. Sit at my desk at 8:00 A.M.
5. Work until 8:55, when I will take a break until 9:05. Repeat this break every hour.
6. Take lunch at 11:55 A.M and be back to work at 12:55 P.M.
7. Stop working at 6:00 P.M.

Roger focused on giving himself a few days and worked on it one step at a time. Once he went to the next step, he rewarded himself with his favorite ice cream treat. When he reached his goal of keeping to his daily schedule for a week ahead of his deadline, he allowed himself to take a vacation day. Roger continues to follow this schedule, and he has found working from home to be more enjoyable as he separates his workday from his personal time with the schedule.

Chapter 5: Yesterday You Said Tomorrow

Scarlett O'Hara from *Gone with the Wind* became famous for saying, "I'll think about that tomorrow," when she came across something that she felt was too difficult or didn't want to think about it when she should (Rice, 2006). While this is often known to bring comic relief into the film, it shows O'Hara's tendency to procrastinate over situations that she should have taken care of at that moment.

Procrastination is when you take extra time to start something or don't focus on a task you should do for several reasons. Everyone procrastinates at some point in their life, and you probably remember several instances when you have procrastinated. For example, you waited until the last minute to start a paper in high school or college. You didn't finish the assigned reading for class, you decided to put off filling your gas tank until the next morning, or you didn't place your dishes in the dishwasher last night because you didn't feel like it.

Procrastination doesn't always cause more problems in our life. For instance, you can do the dishes or fill up your gas tank the following morning, but you might end up running late for work. There are times when procrastination can cause major problems in our life, especially when it comes to not making a deadline at work.

When you let procrastination get out of hand, it can start to harm you emotionally and psychologically. For example, you had three weeks to work on your presentation for work, and now you have two days left. As you look at all the work, you have to do to put your presentation together. You start to mentally scold yourself for waiting so long. You tell yourself that you were stupid for procrastinating, and you had told yourself last time that you wouldn't allow yourself to do this again. You ask yourself why you can't learn from your previous procrastination mistakes. If you didn't make a deadline at work and need to ask for an extension, you deal with anxiety and worry that you will lose your job because you ask for extensions so often due to your procrastination. You ask yourself, "What is wrong with me? Why can't I just get it and do the work as I should? Why don't I know better?"

Procrastination is one of the main roadblocks you have in your life that keep you from making the right decision and reaching your goals. It can keep you from doing what you want, giving you feelings of regret. It can make you feel like you have opportunities slipping away through your fingertips. You don't feel like you are doing anything meaningful and wasting your time. Procrastination is frustrating and causes people to become so angry with themselves that it affects their mindset.

One of the first steps to understanding your procrastination is to know why you procrastinate. This can change from situation to situation. For example, you struggle with anxiety and have to call your bank because you never received a copy of your title once you finished paying off your loan. While you know it isn't your fault, you think of what your previous loan advisor will say. You worry about becoming embarrassed or what will happen if they can't help you. Instead of contacting the bank the day you needed to, you wait another week, always coming up with excuses for why you can't call them day after day. Another reason you find yourself procrastinating is that you don't like the task. You know you need to clean your home, but you are into a show on Netflix, so you continue to watch the show instead of clean. At the end of the day, you look around your home and become frustrated with yourself because you didn't clean like you said you would do that day.

To understand why you procrastinate, you need to assess the situation. Procrastination has a lot to do with your psyche and mindset, while other factors focus more on your personality and environment.

- **You saw your role models procrastinate.** For example, if you struggle with cleaning or making deadlines, ask yourself if you noticed this behavior from your parents, grandparents, or other role models growing up. Try to come up with examples, so you understand where and when you learned to procrastinate.

- **You lack self-confidence.** Self-confidence has a lot to do with procrastination. For example, if you need to write a story for your creative writing class but don't believe that you are a good writer, you will find yourself putting this assignment off as long as possible.

- **You are a perfectionist.** You might not be a perfectionist when it comes to everything, but you feel that it has to be perfect when it comes to the task you are procrastinating on. You continue to put off the task because you don't know how to make it perfect or are afraid you can't make it perfect.

- **You struggle with mental illness.** Mental illness affects several parts of your life. For example, if you have anxiety, you might become anxious when needing to start a new project. Depression will cause procrastination because you are not interested in the project. Mental illness diminishes your concentration and motivation.

- **You can't focus because you aren't comfortable in your environment.** Are you trying to focus on the task but find yourself looking around your environment and thinking about how it isn't comfortable? For example, you don't feel

it is clean enough, or it feels cramped.
- **You feel scared.** If you need to perform a new task, you might procrastinate because you don't know how you will do it. For example, you received a promotion at work. You know that you are a good fit and you are confident in your abilities, but you are scared about what your co-workers and supervisors will think about your work.

Remove Temptations

Roger works from home, and he is trying to focus on writing a book for one of his clients. The due date is fast approaching, and Roger is afraid he won't make the deadline. While he is working diligently on the project, the topic is more difficult than his other topics. He also finds himself distracted every time he hears his phone. He feels like he has to answer his phone, even when it is a message on his personal social media accounts.

Roger has tried to ignore his phone by putting his ringer and notifications on silent, but he found himself checking his phone every five minutes as he worried he would miss an important message from a client. Roger tried to place his work app on a different notification sound and only pay attention to this notification tone during work hours, but he still found himself checking his phone. He even tried to leave his phone in a separate room to use the "out of sight, out of mind" concept, but he found himself checking his phone every 15 minutes.

To remove the temptation of checking his phone, Roger downloaded his work app onto his computer. He then shut off his phone and placed it in another room. At first, Roger found himself thinking about checking his phone and walking up to turn his phone on every half hour. However, after a couple of days, Roger started to have his phone off and away from him while working. He went from checking his phone every half hour to once an hour. Soon, he was only checking his phone during his breaks.

Like most of us, Roger struggled with removing temptations that kept him from working. Temptations are one of the main reasons for procrastination, and it is difficult to remove the temptations as this involves strong self-discipline.

Breaking free of your temptations is sometimes the hardest part about overcoming procrastination and developing your self-discipline. Temptations can be like food cravings for your brain—you need to have them. Because of this, you can treat the temptations that cause you to procrastinate like a craving. For example, you can limit your access. This is what Roger did when he turned his phone off and placed it in another room. Doing this made him think twice about whether he really needed to stop working, get up, walk to his cell phone, turn it on, and wait so he could check it. If your temptation is watching television when you should be working, you can place your remotes somewhere so it is more difficult to turn on the television. You can also work in an area where there is no television.

Another way to break free of your temptations is to use the 15 minutes rule. You commit to not allowing yourself to give in to your temptation for 15 minutes. The method to this rule is by the time 15 minutes have passed, your brain is no longer focused on your temptation, and you continue to work on your project instead.

Learn to Say No

One of the most difficult words to say for many people is "no." You often feel bad for telling someone that you can't help them with a task or that you feel you need a reason to say no. First, you never need a reason to say 'no' as this word is a sentence all by itself. Second, you should never feel bad about putting yourself first and knowing what you can and cannot handle.

When it comes to your temptation, saying no is different because you aren't telling another person no unless they ask you to go to the movies with them instead of focusing on your task. You are most likely telling yourself no when it comes to your temptations. This should be easier, right? No. In fact, it can be harder to say no to your temptations than to another person.

One of the ways to tell yourself no is by focusing on the difference between "I won't" and "I can't." The difference is your mindset when it comes to the two phrases. When you say "I won't," it implies that you choose not to do something. When you say "I can't," it makes you feel like there is another force stopping you from making the decision, and this can cause you to give in to your temptation more. In other words, saying "I won't" gives you more power over the situation.

For example, you are increasing the amount of time you exercise every day. You are finding yourself saying, "I can't go another 10 minutes because I am too sore and tired." Instead of saying this, tell yourself, "I am not the type of person to end their workout early," meaning you won't end your workout early. If you find yourself sleeping in late in the morning, tell yourself that you are not the type of person to sleep in as you know it's a waste of time.

Plan of Action

There are many strategies you can follow when creating a plan of action to overcome your temptations. You might feel inspired by the strategies you read here or create your own. If you are stuck when it comes to creating a plan of action, you can focus on these steps as inspiration.

1. **Set a date.** It is important to set a date to focus on avoiding temptation. Setting a date helps you prepare for the change in your routine or prepares your mind to know that you will focus on avoiding your temptation starting at a certain time. When you set a time, you will become more successful in your efforts.
2. **Write down the reasons why.** You are more likely to resist your temptation if you understand why you want to avoid it. For example, Roger decided to avoid his phone because it was causing him to fall behind in his work. He wasn't focusing when he was writing because he was always mindful of when his phone gave a tone.
3. **Visualize your end result.** Imagine yourself succeeding in avoiding your temptation. For example, Roger imagined that he had improved his workflow and didn't need to worry about asking for extensions for his deadlines because he could concentrate on his work instead of his phone.
4. **What to do when your temptation increases?** There are some temptations that you can't completely remove from your environment. When this happens, you need to have a plan in place on what you will do if your temptation increases and you think about giving in. For example, you can find something different to do. If you feel that you are thinking about your temptation because you need a break

from your task, take a break but do something different. Roger is trying to stay away from Netflix during the day because he can't watch just one episode of his favorite television show. This causes him to fall behind on his work. Therefore, when he needs a break, he decides to go for a short walk or read his book instead of watching Netflix.

Create the Right Environment

Creating the right environment means looking around you to see what keeps you from achieving your goals and focusing on your tasks. For example, if you work from home, it is best to create an office area. Even if you have a laptop, do your best to work in one spot as this will condition your mind to know that it is time to work when you sit at your desk.

You also want to look beyond your office and home walls. Notice who you hang out with and call your friends. Are they helping you achieve your goals, or do they slow you down? If people don't support you, then it is time to let them go. You want to distance yourself from them as much as possible. It is important to have people in your life who support your goals and dreams, as this will help you become more successful.

It isn't easy to let people go who don't have your best interest at heart. It is important to remember that you don't have to end the relationship completely — and you always need to be honest with them. First, try to communicate with the person. Tell them what you have noticed, as they might not understand your goals or their actions. They might try to focus more on supporting you. However, if you don't notice a change in their behavior, you need to limit contact with them.

Strategies to Help You Overcome Procrastination

We discussed removing temptations and creating the right environment separately, as those are the two biggest strategies to help you overcome procrastination. There are many other strategies that people use we will discuss in this section.

It is important to note that you can use any strategy you are comfortable with. You might find yourself using more than one strategy, and you might find that you only need one strategy at a time. What you choose is directly up to you. You need to make sure that you are comfortable with it, yet you need to keep yourself a little uncomfortable to continue to achieve your goals.

Find a Mentor

You want to seek out someone who has already overcome their struggles with procrastination. They can help you through the process and be a sense of support that will allow you to feel that you can achieve your goal, especially when you find yourself struggling to do so. There will always be days when you feel that your steps and goal are easier than other days. During the difficult days, you will need someone, or several people, on your side to give you support to keep going. Your mentor will be the main person and never let you give up. They will work with you through any struggles that you have and help you reevaluate your goals if needed.

Don't Overcomplicate Anything

It is easy to overthink and make situations more complicated than they are, especially when trying to reach goals. You might feel that you can't start on a certain day because it is not the right time. You might continue to push your goal back because you don't feel that you have the right mindset to start focusing on your goals. All of the problems and excuses you use to justify putting off your goal make everything more complicated. For example, Roger wanted to focus on his goal of getting up at 6:00 A.M. for months as this allowed him two hours to relax in the morning before work. The problem was that Roger would continue to relax in bed and kept telling himself he would hit "snooze" as this was relaxing. Suddenly, Roger noticed it was 7:30 A.M, and he was about to be late for work.

Once Roger started working from home, he continued to hit snooze until almost 8:00 A.M. or later because he made his own hours. This caused problems because Roger had less energy to focus on work when he slept in so late. He would find himself working slowly or becoming easily distracted until 1:00 in the afternoon. It was at this time he would start to kick himself for not working earlier on his project. Roger's emotions toward himself created more complications for his mindset, making him struggle to stick to his schedule more.

You might over-complicate matters when you feel that the situation needs to be perfect. Not only do you need to start at a certain time, but you have to know a certain amount of information, your office area needs to be perfect, and you need to work without making any mistakes. When this happens, you allow your perfectionism to take control. You always need to remember that nothing is perfect. You do the best job you can do, learn from your mistakes, and move on. Once you realize what you can control and what you can't, you start to focus on what you can control, and situations become less complicated. This also helps with your mindset, as you are less likely to become frustrated with your mistakes.

Break Your Work into Small Steps

The struggle people have when it comes to their goals is looking at it as one big picture, which is why it is important to break your goals into smaller steps. You want to take the same action when you focus on the work you feel is too daunting, even if it is your whole workday.

Roger knew that starting his writing and editing business and working from home meant that he wouldn't have a typical 9 to 5 office-type job. Some days he would work 12 or more hours, and other days he would work eight or less. Roger also understood that there could be times he worked during the weekend and didn't take a day off for weeks. He was prepared to take on this schedule. However, once he started working from home, he began to feel overwhelmed and found himself procrastinating worse than ever.

Besides creating a schedule and limiting his distractions, Roger's mentor told him to break his workday down into smaller steps just as he does his goals. At first, Roger wasn't sure how to go about this task. He couldn't comprehend how to break down his workday, as he would just be writing and editing throughout the day. This was when his mentor stepped in to help him. First, Roger needed to write down everything he did in one day.

He wrote:

- Check email and direct messages.
- Research
- Write

- Edit
- Look for other work once a project is complete

To help Roger develop a complete list, his mentor asked him how he manages his projects. Roger says he only allows himself to have four to five projects at a time because he knows he can work for an hour and a half to two hours on each project every day. Therefore, Roger's mentor told him to include each project in his phases. Roger created a new list that looked like the following:

- Check email and direct messages
- Work on project one from 8:00 to 10:30 A.M.
- Work on project two from 10:30 A.M. to 11:55 A.M.
- Work on project three from 12:55 A.M. to 2:30 P.M.
- Work on project four from 2:30 P.M. to 4:00 P.M.
- If I have a project five, work on that from 4:00 P.M. to 5:30 P.M.
- If I don't have a fifth project, work on the project that is due first.
- Finish up the day between 5:30 to 6:00 P.M.

Once Roger's day was broken down into steps, he could focus on one step at a time. This helped Roger feel more comfortable managing his projects and gave him more motivation to complete his tasks. Roger found that when he worked on one project at a time, he became bored with the project. He would become more distracted in the afternoon as he felt he needed a break from the project, but he knew he had to continue. If he took a break, he usually took a long break because it was hard for him to get motivated to sit back at his desk. By working on four to five projects in a day, Roger knows he is making progress on each project every day, and he doesn't become distracted easily.

Chapter 6: Increase Your Self-Confidence

"With realization of one's own potential and self-confidence in one's ability, one can build a better world."

– Dalai Lama

We have already discussed what self-confidence is, so now it is time to look at how you can improve your self-confidence through various strategies. One factor to remember is that as you are working on your self-discipline, even if it is only in one area of your life, you are naturally improving your self-confidence. Once you build your self-confidence in one area of your life, you will start to feel more confident in other areas of your life.

When Roger started writing, he didn't have a lot of self-confidence in his abilities. He felt that he was a good writer, but he didn't believe his writing would take him anywhere. He didn't believe that he could support himself and his family with a writing career, even though this is what he wanted to do. Roger had always loved writing, ever since he was a young child, but he didn't have many people tell him that he was good at writing. In fact, his parents told him that he couldn't go anywhere with his writing and that he should decide on another career.

The first job Roger received as a freelance writer was for a small article about Thanksgiving. His client loved the article but never got in touch with him to write another article. Roger received jobs from online blogs, but most were on a volunteer basis. About nine months into his freelance career, Roger thought about giving up and sticking with his office job. However, he received a position as a writer for a ghostwriting company. Roger wasn't positive that he could give them the high-quality writing they wanted, but he decided to give it a try.

Within two months, Roger became one of the company's top writers. His supervisors praised his work and told him that he was an amazing writer. He received great reviews from the editors but still struggled to believe that he was a good writer. As Roger continued to develop as a writer, he continued to improve his writing. At the same time, his self-confidence as a writer improved. Within six months on the job, Roger left his employer and created his own writing company. He started writing full-time at home and knew he would continue to improve as a writer. Roger started to believe what his editors and supervisors told him about his writing, which improved his self-confidence on the job.

Over time, Roger noted that his self-confidence also improved in his personal life. He believed that he could learn new tasks. He started to focus on hobbies that he previously didn't believe he could accomplish. He began to hold conversations with people he barely knew and confidently told them his opinions and thoughts, even if the other people didn't agree with him. Because of the confidence, Roger gained from his job as a writer. He gained confidence in other areas of his life.

How to Build Your Self-Confidence

It is important to note that no one has a limit when it comes to self-confidence. You are not born with only 10% of self-confidence or the ability to grow your self-confidence to 25%. People who exhibit strong self-confidence have worked on building their confidence for years. Even if they grew up in a loving home with supportive and encouraging parents, they still worked on building their self-confidence when they left home. Self-confidence is a part of your mindset that you will constantly develop.

There is no right or wrong limit when it comes to self-confidence. Some people are afraid to act confident about their abilities because they worry they will seem narcissistic or arrogant to someone. Someone with strong self-confidence is not narcissistic. Narcissism is a personality disorder that causes people to believe they are the best at everything. They believe there is no one better than them, and they will do anything in their power to remain on top — even hurting other people. Self-confidence shines in people and makes them more likely to help other people. They want to see other people succeed, just as they have succeeded. They work hard and understand that they will continue to improve their skills. They know they can learn from other people and are willing to do what they can to ensure they help themselves and others.

There are many strategies you can use when you work on building your self-confidence. You might find yourself starting with one strategy and looking into a new strategy only once you have more self-confidence. This happens because as your self-confidence grows, your methods will also develop. You will start to focus on other areas of your life, or you will start to notice you need to build on certain personality traits, which takes different strategies. No matter where you sit with your self-confidence, here are a few strategies that you can incorporate into your life.

Use Affirmations

One of the biggest ways people start to increase their self-confidence is through affirmations. These are uplifting and positive sayings that you can read wherever you are, through books or by Googling positive or motivational quotes. When you use affirmations to build your self-confidence, you want to focus on quotes that will lift your spirits. For example, if you are struggling with your job, you can look at quotes more specific in your field of study or quotes that focus on any career.

You always want to say the affirmation out loud. You can read it in your mind first, but you will believe the message more if you read it aloud.

Take a moment to say the following quote in your head:

"The best way to predict the future is to create it."
- Abraham Lincoln

Now, take time to reflect on how that quote made you feel. Did you think much about it, or did you read it like you read anything else? People often read quotes in their minds like they will read a novel. While they can feel the quote bringing them a sense of peace or creating more positivity, it doesn't last long. In fact, it only lasts a matter of seconds for most people.

Now, take a moment to say the following quote out loud:

"The most important thing is to look ahead. The past is your anchor."

- Maxime Lagace

Once again, reflect on what you read out loud. Did you notice any difference from when you read Abraham Lincoln's quote in your head? Did you find yourself thinking about Maxime Lagace's quote more than Lincoln's quote? Most people will notice that they not only take the quote more seriously when they read it out loud, but it sticks in their minds longer. They focus more on the meaning of the quote and how it relates to them.

Another trick to affirmations is to remain consistent. The more often you speak a quote, the more you will believe what you are reading. You don't need to read the same quote over and over again. You can always read a new quote, but it should be positive. The more positive quotes you read throughout your day, the stronger your self-confidence will become. Because you start to feel more positive mentally, you will start to become more positive emotionally. Your mental and emotional positivity will radiate into physical positivity, making you feel better overall.

You don't have to read other people's positive quotes to get yourself to focus on affirmations. You can focus on your own affirmations by looking at the areas in your life where you want to build your confidence. The key is to say them in a way that is a question. This is because your brain naturally wants to seek out answers to questions. For example, during her college years, Amirah noticed professors praised her written papers and essay questions. They told her she was an excellent writer, which is something Amirah had never thought about before. In fact, she never wanted to become a writer. But she knew that she needed to use this as a tool to help build her mental toughness and mindset. So, she asked herself, "Why am I a good writer?" instead of telling herself, "I am a good writer."

Take a moment to think about an area where you want to improve your self-confidence. This could be at your job, school, or your mindset. Then, tell yourself what you are good at by saying, "I am good at ____." Now, it is time to turn that statement into a question. Ask yourself, "Why am I good at ____." Reflect on how you continue to think about this question as your brain is trying to find an answer. You might come up with a few reasons why you are good at the task within a few minutes or might find yourself continuing to think about the question throughout the day. Take time at the end of your day to reflect on the exercise.

Imagine What You Want to Become

Since you were younger, you wanted to become someone. You might remember who you wanted to become in kindergarten, such as a teacher, firefighter, police officer, or animal. Children have wild imaginations but believe that anything they imagine is possible. The main reason for this is that they visualize themselves as what they want to be. For example, if you wanted to be a firefighter, you imagined yourself fighting a house fire and becoming a hero. As a teacher, it would be teaching a class and enjoying your time with your students.

Unfortunately, using the visualization technique pushes people off to the side like a child's play. Older children, teenagers, and adults shouldn't visualize like children because people are meant to outgrow this stage, right? Wrong. This is one of the biggest myths when it comes to self-confidence. The truth is, the more you visualize who you want to become, the stronger your confidence grows in that area. Of course, confidence is a snowball effect, which means that once it begins to develop in one area, it will develop in other areas. You might not notice this development, but one day you will reflect on where you were a year ago and where you are now and notice your growth, which will astound you.

Sometimes people need help with visualization, and this is fine. There is nothing wrong with creating a visualization board that shows pictures of your goals and where you see yourself within a year. Creating a vision board is easy and cheap. You can cut pictures from magazines and glue them onto a cardboard backing or print off pictures related to your goals and glue them. You can also draw pictures and use quotes or specific words that help you stay focused on your goals.

You want to place your vision board somewhere in your home so that you will see it every day. It is important that you spend time reflecting on your vision board in the morning or before you go to bed for at least 10 minutes every day. Look carefully at the pictures and think about your progress with each image.

Many people like to include journaling with their vision boards. As they reflect, they will discuss the steps they completed that day to help them reach their goals. Journaling is beneficial because it allows you to think about what you have accomplished. For example, if you are having a tough day and feel that your self-confidence is a little lower than normal, you can look through your journal and notice all the improvements you have made over a certain period.

Help Someone Else

Many people focus on building their self-confidence by helping someone else. This person can be a friend, family member, or stranger. You might find yourself volunteering at a local nonprofit, such as a food pantry, or setting up a drive for people who are in the middle of a natural disaster. You might decide you will help one person every day and make this part of your routine. No matter what you decide to do, helping someone else is a guaranteed way to build up your self-confidence because it makes you feel good.

Take a moment to think about a time when you helped someone. No matter who the person is, remember how you felt after you knew you helped them. If you need to, take time to remind yourself of the situation and then allow your feelings to come to you naturally. As you think about the moment, your emotions will start to come to the surface.

One of the reasons why helping someone helps us build our self-confidence is because we forget about ourselves for a moment. We don't think about our troubles. Instead, we become more grateful for what we have in life. We start to see our lives differently. This means that the more you help someone, the stronger your self-confidence will become as you will continue to feel blessed in your life.

For example, you tend to focus on your weaknesses and believe that you can't become the person you want to become. You are working on becoming your best self, a person who believes they will succeed, can save money, works hard, doesn't procrastinate and can control their emotions. However, you find yourself struggling to reach even a part of the person you want to become. This all starts to change when you walk into your church one Sunday and see a group of women sewing. You ask them what they are doing, and they tell you that they are knitting and sewing scarves, hats, and gloves to ship to people all over the world to stay warm during the winter. You then ask how you can become a part of this process, and they tell you to join them anytime.

Even though you don't know anything about sewing or knitting, they take the time to help you. Soon, you are a part of a group that is shipping six boxes filled with winter items to children in Alaska. You smile as you see the boxes leave the church and the UPS truck drive off. As you think about this process, you realize how much you believe in yourself because you are helping children stay warm during the winter months.

Do One Thing that Scares You Every Day

Like most people, you want to stay away from the factors that scare you. You don't want to face fears because it is uncomfortable, and you never know what will happen. For example, if you want to go on a haunted house tour for Halloween, but you are scared about the setup, from people dressed as Zombies to people jumping out, you are more than likely going to stay away from haunted houses. You might worry about screaming when someone jumps out at you, and people will think that you are stupid or too scared to handle a situation like this. Even though you want to go with your friends to a haunted house every Halloween, you come up with a reason why you can't go every year. Other risks that might scare you include getting started on your own business, picking up a new hobby, or cleaning out your storage closet because you haven't been there for years.

As you plan your day, you want to think about one thing that scares you. This could make you feel uncomfortable, something that gives you anxiety when you think about it, or something that makes you want to run and hide. As you focus on your morning routine, write down the one item you will do that day that you are afraid of. Doing something every day that puts a little fear in you helps you become comfortable with being uncomfortable. It builds your confidence because you start to realize your potential. Instead of telling yourself, "I can't do that" or "That sounds a bit scary," you tell yourself, "I did it."

Set Yourself Up to Win

Not only do you want to focus on setting up for your goal, but you also want to make sure you set yourself up to win. This means you don't want to make your goals or steps hard to achieve. You want to make them easy, yet you don't want them to be too easy. At the same time, it is important to remember that steps might look too easy when you write them down on paper. For example, setting a goal to get up at 7:00 in the morning can seem easy and not challenging at all. However, when you are in the habit of sleeping in until 8:00 A.M. or don't get up to an alarm, the step is a little harder, especially if you don't have strong self-discipline to get up when your alarm goes off. People can hit snooze several times or turn their alarm off and then easily fall back asleep. You want to avoid this when you are setting your goals and trying to stick to them.

Another way to set yourself up to win is to make your first two steps easier than your other steps. For example, you can increase the difficulty of each step of your goal. This will help you get a start with your goals and then keep you motivated and give you a little extra challenge with each step. This can help you overcome any discomfort you have with your goal or become a part of doing one thing that scares you. It is always possible to combine two strategies at the same time.

When You are Struggling, Look at What You Have Already Achieved

Everyone has moments when they become frustrated with their goals, and you are no different. You might feel that you can't reach your goal because you continue to make a mistake during one step, or you don't think to feel that you set your goal too high. You might have a bad day and don't have any energy to focus on your goals, even if it is a part of your daily routine. Roger finds himself struggling when one of his clients requests a revision. Even though the clients asked Roger to switch a few things around and tell him, they loved his writing and appreciated how much work he put into the book. He still feels like he made a mistake and disappointed his client with the revision. Roger understands that his clients are excited to receive their finished product and want to send it to publication as soon as they receive it. He knows having to wait for revisions can set them back a few days.

Roger used to find himself taking revisions so hard that it became difficult for him to focus on his work for the rest of the day. There were times that he felt he couldn't focus on his work the next day because he kept thinking about the revision he needed to do. This caused Roger to fall behind on his goal setting, which mentally and emotionally made matters worse for Roger.

Roger talked to his mentor to help himself stay out of a downward spiral when he received a revision. Roger's mentor told him that revisions are a part of the ghostwriting business. If he received any bad reviews or comments, he should reevaluate his work and see if the client's comments are justified. Roger's mentor stated that while they usually are, you can't please everyone, and you need to be prepared for the client who will never be truly happy with their project. The mentor also told Roger that he should take any other revisions as to what they are. If a client loves the work but wants a few things changed, then you make those changes.

Since Roger accepted that there were revisions for his business, he became more comfortable when he received one. He understood that it was an opportunity for growth and not something he should be ashamed of. Instead of struggling with the revision, Roger would go back and read the positive comments he received from his clients. It helped to lift his spirits, so he didn't back away from his work. In fact, Roger found that he became more motivated to make the projects even better when he received revisions.

Chapter 7: Build Willpower

When you have strong willpower, you control your impulses. You know what you need to do to reach your goal or get the job done. Willpower is an important part of self-discipline because it helps you focus on what you need to do instead of what you want to do.

Everyone has some type of willpower. You might have the willpower to help you get tasks done when you are close to your deadline. You might find that your willpower is stronger when you first receive your task and get it started than when you are approaching the deadline. While some people can tell themselves "no" easily and follow through with their decision, other people don't have that strong willpower and find themselves bending to their desires.

Two Main Parts of Building Willpower

There are two main parts when it comes to building willpower. The first part is motivation, and the second part is tracking your progress. Through these two factors, your willpower will slowly build and help you stay on track with your goals.

Before we discuss the two main parts, it is important to take time to discuss consistency. You need to make sure that you follow through with your plan whenever working on willpower. For example, you want to have some type of tracking system that shows the progress you have made for every goal you set. Your goal setting and tracking system will become more of a habit by remaining consistent in these efforts than something you need to do. You will want to follow through with the system because you understand the benefits, and you know what the outcome will be if you continue to remain consistent.

An example of how important consistency is and what it can do for you is the story of Samantha. As a freshman in college, Samantha struggled to make her classes. She felt that because everyone posted the work online and attendance was not part of her grade, she didn't need to go to class all the time. Instead, she would go to class if she needed to hand in an assignment and talk to her professor because she was having a problem understanding her classwork or a test or quiz. Samantha also told herself that if she found her grades were lower than a B, she would go to the class until her grades improved, and then she could start to miss classes again.

Because Samantha found herself missing so many class periods, she didn't meet many new people. When she did show up to class, she felt out of place and that everyone knew she hadn't been in class lately. She felt that the professor judged her for only coming to class on certain days. She started to believe that no one thought she would graduate from college.

Because Samantha missed so many classes, it quickly became a habit. She soon found herself missing important days, such as a day a quiz was scheduled because she didn't remember when her classes were. Soon, Samantha's habit was of missing classes instead of going to classes. At the end of the semester, Samantha received word that she was on academic probation and would be kicked out of school if she didn't improve her grade point average to 2.5.

After talking to her older sister, Samantha realized that her willpower to go to class diminished because she rarely went. Therefore, she felt it took more energy to go to class than to stay home and complete the assignments online or give her professor an excuse that she wasn't feeling well so she could make up a quiz. Samantha's sister told her that she needs to consistently go to class to build her motivation for her classes. Once she became more motivated, she would find that she wanted to make it to her classes.

The next semester Samantha made it a goal to miss classes for an emergency or when she was sick. She wrote it down in her planner whenever she made the class, and when she struggled to find the energy to go to class, Samantha looked back at her planner to see that she hadn't missed a class yet. Feeling proud of herself, she continued to go to class. By the fourth week of class, Samantha felt she had to get to class. When she came down with the flu in the sixth week, she felt bad for missing class and struggled to stay home and take care of herself instead of going to class.

For Samantha, remaining consistent in going to class and tracking the days she went to class kept her motivated to continue the process. At the end of the semester, Samantha found herself on the Dean's List and rarely missed a class during the remainder of her college career.

Motivating Yourself

It is true. It is easy to motivate other people. It is hard to motivate yourself because it is easier to tell yourself, "I can do this later, I will have time," or "I can think about this tomorrow when I feel better and more motivated. Everyone deserves a day off." It is easier to listen to someone when they tell you to remain motivated or go to class because you don't want to disappoint them. You want your parents, friends, siblings, or significant others to be proud of you. Therefore, you tend to listen to their requests over your own.

Motivating yourself is an important part of your daily life. You need to motivate yourself to get up when your alarm goes off. You need to motivate yourself to make supper after a busy day. You need to motivate yourself to work instead of surfing the internet. You probably don't even realize all the times you need to motivate yourself throughout the day.

There are several techniques you can use to help motivate yourself:

1. **Get Positive.** It is easier for other people to motivate you because they are excited and positive. Some people feel silly when they try to make themselves feel excited and positive about a task they need to take on. However, it is essential to help get yourself motivated. The more excited and positive you are about completing the task, the more motivation you will have to focus on the task. Give yourself a pep talk if you need to. You can stand in front of the mirror to do this or talk to yourself out loud.

2. **Surround yourself with people that will pressure you.** Talk to people, such as your friends and family, about your goals. Ask them if they will be your sense of support when you are working on the task. If they want to see you

succeed, they will agree to be your support. Tell them that there will be times they need to pressure you to get the job done or make sure that you are on track with your progress.

3. **Always give yourself rewards.** Once you complete a step or a task, reward yourself. The reward is there to keep you motivated, so you continue working on the next part of your task or move on to a new goal.

4. **Get started, as the motivation will come.** You might be one of those people who find motivation once they get a project started. If you like to see a project through to the end, it might be helpful to start the project and then look for your motivation. Chances are, you will find it as now that you have started the project, you need to make sure you finish it.

5. **Get motivated through music.** If you are the type of person that likes to work with background noise, you might find yourself more motivated to work when you have some of your favorite songs playing in the background. It is important to analyze if music will really help you with motivation and what type of music. For example, Amirah can concentrate on a task while listening to some of her favorite songs. At the same time, Roger finds himself becoming distracted as he would rather listen

to music than work. Therefore, Roger listens to classical or relaxing music that plays softly in the background.

6. **Compare yourself to yourself.** Like most people, you are probably good at comparing yourself to other people. You see your co-workers working hard at their tasks and wonder why you don't have this motivation yourself. You compare yourself to your friends who have more money, a bigger home, and nicer cars. You wonder why you can't get to that point and if it is because you don't work as hard. Instead of comparing yourself to other people, it is time to compare yourself to yourself. Look at your progress and think about the person you used to be when you first started the job. For example, Roger didn't have the confidence as a writer when he first started that he does now. Because of this confidence, Roger has become a stronger writer. When Roger compares himself, he notices how far he has come and can't help but become more motivated to continue his path.

Recording Your Progress

There are different ways to track your progress, and it is important to focus on a method that works for you. The key is to be consistent with your method, as this will keep you motivated to record your progress on a task every day. You can use one of the methods discussed below, or you can create your own method. You want to do something that is comfortable and will work with your lifestyle. For example, Roger doesn't have to worry about getting ready for bed or putting the kids to bed, so he records his progress after his evening meal. Amirah has a hectic schedule that often takes her away at certain times of the day. She doesn't always know when she will be home and when she won't, so she records her progress right before she goes to bed.

- **Start at zero but set a daily goal.** This method helps when you are trying to increase your exercise or walk many miles a day. The key is to always start at zero and try to reach a daily goal. For example, if you have a Fitbit, you have a certain number of steps you want to reach every day. At midnight, your watch starts at zero and records every step you make throughout the day. When you reach your goal, your watch makes a noise or vibrates, letting you know that your goal is met. This is the same idea you want to follow with other goals. For instance, you want to exercise for 30 more minutes every day. You will start at zero and then see how many minutes you exercised by the end of each day. You will record this progress in a journal or through a data tracker.

- **Journaling.** One of the most common methods of tracking progress is to write in a journal. You don't have to spend a lot of time writing in a journal every day. Most people can detail their progress within five minutes. However, it is important to take the time to write about your progress, even if you are more tired than usual or don't feel like writing that evening. You don't want to put it off until morning because you could forget to write down important tracking information, and you get out of your system. You can keep this journal as your tracking journal, but if you are working on more than one goal, you want to make sure you separate your goals into different sections. You don't want to write about different goals on the same page, as this can become confusing when you look back at your progress.
- **Excel spreadsheet, or Microsoft Word.** Another way you can track your progress is by creating an excel spreadsheet or using Microsoft word. Doing this allows you to create a document that works for your system and keep it updated when you are on your computer. For example, you might find the best time to track your work progress is at the end of your workday.

There are four main steps when it comes to tracking your progress, no matter what method you use:

1. **Look at the bigger picture.** When you go through your day, you often follow the same pattern. This can lead to mindless thoughts and keep you from focusing on what you need to do. When you look at the big picture as you track your goals, you ask yourself a series of questions, such as "What do I want to accomplish?" and "What do I need to do to get my day started?" By thinking about these questions, you will visualize the result you want. This will get you started focusing on your tasks and help you know what factors you need to consider when you are tracking your progress.

2. **Organize and plan your time.** Get a planner to help you stay on track with your goals. Write down what you want to achieve every day when it comes to your goals. Even if you only want to achieve calling your friends to see if they will become a source of motivation, you want to write this down. After all, part of reaching your goals is to have a support network. When you know how long it should take you to reach your milestones, write them in your planner. For example, if you want to get to the second milestone in 10 days, write this down.

3. **Don't do this alone.** You need to find a partner that wants to focus on the same goal or someone that will be your accountability partner. This person can help you stay on track by motivating you to continue and helping you understand your progress. They can look to see where you are with your progress and notice if you are on track or not.
4. **Remember to celebrate your success.** You want to write down your celebrations just as you make your progress.

You Will Feel Drained

You don't want to read that a task you are taking on will make you feel drained. However, you must understand that working toward self-development can make you feel overwhelmed even when you focus on small steps. You will have moments where you want to throw in the towel because you don't think you can accomplish your goal. You will have moments when your self-confidence seems low because you start bringing yourself down with your thoughts about how you aren't on track with your goal and you are a failure.

Emotions and mental work drain us, and working toward a goal is mental and emotional work. You don't have to have a labor-intensive job to feel tired at the end of a workday. People who have a mentally intensive job can feel just as drained as people with a physically intensive job. It is not a competition, and you should never feel that you don't work as hard as someone who works in construction.

Another way working toward self-discipline is draining is because you are trying to better yourself. This requires a lot of focus and more work than you are used to. Even though recording your progress might only take five to ten minutes out of your day, you can feel drained when you need to reflect on your day every evening.

You must realize the effort and focus you put toward your self-discipline and all its step is draining, but this should not scare you away. If it does, this should give you more motivation to focus on developing your self-discipline.

No matter how drained you feel at the end of the day, you have made progress and have increased your self-discipline. This is one reason why tracking your progress is so important. It helps you stay focused, especially during the tough days when you feel like you aren't making any progress.

If you go through a day where you don't focus on your progress, you don't have to take this to heart. Everyone has days when trying to find motivation is harder than any other task that day. Instead of emotionally and mentally beating yourself up over it, you want to think about it as a mental health day of progress. You needed a break, which everyone does from time to time. Take your mental health day and focus on reenergizing yourself for the next phase in mastering your self-discipline.

You Must Be Willing to Fail

Failing is not easy, especially when you are focused on a task and want to do your best. However, you need to remember that you can't have success without failures. When you fail, this allows you to learn and grow. The key when it comes to failures is to fall forward. This means that you will use the opportunity to improve your weaknesses and learn from your mistakes. Even some of the most well-known movie stars received rejections, especially in their early days. Some of them have movies that didn't make it to the big screen, while others are open about the failures they have had in their careers. Remember, when you fail, you are not alone in this process as everyone fails at some point in their lives — many times throughout their lives at that.

Chapter 8: Control Your Mind

Becoming the master of your mind takes a lot of willpower, focus, and determination. However, it is essential to master your self-discipline. You always want to remember that the best tool you have to give yourself a better life and reach your best self is your mind. This means you need to be in control of your thoughts to reach your self-discipline mastery.

The first step you need to take when it comes to taking control of your mind is to know your inner critic. This is the part of you that wants to drag you down and gives you your most unhealthy thoughts. Your inner critic develops throughout your life. It developed from people who told you that you wouldn't succeed, through your parents when they criticized you, through bullies, and from comparing yourself to other people. It is important to remember that your inner critic is you. You are the one who is thinking about these negative thoughts and sometimes emotionally and mentally abusing yourself. It is time to face yourself and realize that if you wouldn't treat anyone else this way, why should you treat yourself in this manner. Start to silence your inner critic.

You might have other parts of yourself that you need to learn to let go of before you can truly take control of your mind. For example, if you have anxiety and excessive worry, you need to overcome this worry to gain control of your mind. One technique to help manage anxiety or worry is to think of this piece of you as a little person or monster sitting on your shoulder. You can decorate the little person however you want. For example, you can imagine it looking like an ugly troll. The troll whispers worries and anxieties into your ear, which makes you focus on them instead of what you should be focusing on - developing your self-discipline. When you are anxious or worried and hear these thoughts, take control of them by telling your anxiety troll that she is not right. Instead, tell the troll what is true. For instance, if your troll tells you that you will fail your exam, tell her that you won't because you are intelligent, studied, and confident you know the material. As you are telling your troll the truth, imagine it getting smaller and smaller with each word. Eventually, your troll is so small, and its voice is so tiny and squeaky that you don't have any more anxiety about your exam.

Maintaining Focus

Once you have let go of your struggles, such as anxiety and your inner critic, you can start to improve your focus. There are several strategies that you can use to improve your focus. You want to find the best methods for yourself. However, there are many strategies that everyone should follow, as they will help you maintain your focus throughout the day.

Start Your Morning with a Routine

There are many ways to start your morning off with a routine. You might find yourself in the kitchen, making coffee. Once you have about half of a cup of coffee, you head to get ready for the day. From there, you decide that you will take 10 minutes to do something that helps you become more focused on your day. For example, you will meditate, read, or exercise. You might try several methods before you settle on one that helps you maintain your focus best throughout the day.

Focus on Good Fats in Your Food

There are tons of diets globally, but some of the most popular focus on limiting carbohydrates and getting more healthy fats into your body. For example, many people are starting to follow the Ketogenic diet. They eat so many healthy fats throughout the day that their body starts using fats to burn energy instead of carbohydrates. This makes people feel more energized and improves their focus naturally. If you are looking for a diet, as losing weight and eating healthier is one of your goals, you should look into a diet that focuses more on healthy fats than eating smaller portions.

Keep an Hour by Hour Planner

There are several types of planners that you can find in stores. You can get a planner that looks like a wall calendar or one that gives you more room to write down your main tasks during your day. You can also find planners that are broken down into hours. Many people feel the best planner to choose is a motivational planner that will list the hours as this allows you to write down your main task for every hour. Roger takes four to five projects at once and likes to work on all of them throughout the day. Therefore, he found the hourly planner to be the best fit for him because he can write down the project he is working on and even his breaks to help him keep to his schedule.

Get Enough Sleep

Getting enough sleep is often a tip for focusing that is overlooked. Like most people, you have a busy life, and it seems that every minute of every day is accounted for. This means that you sometimes find yourself staying up later at night so you can relax by watching a movie. Unfortunately, this cuts down on the amount of sleep you get that night, affecting you the following day and making it harder for you to maintain your focus. Even if you feel that you should complete a task that night, you want to set a bedtime and stick to it so you can make sure to get at least 7 to 8 hours of good sleep every night.

Meditation

One of the most popular forms of controlling your mind is meditation. Like most people, once you start meditating, you will quickly find the benefits that allow you to maintain focus, control your mind, control your emotions, and improve your mental and emotional health, further improving your physical health.

There are different types of meditation, and you can focus on any type. But, because it is helpful to be mindful when you are building your self-discipline, it is best to focus on mindfulness meditation. You want to set aside at least 10 minutes every day for meditation. Most people focus on this in the morning, as meditation helps clear your mind and gets you more motivated for your day. However, this can be tough for some people, especially if there are small children because you need to limit distractions so you can focus well. Many parents find it best to get up about half an hour earlier than the rest of their family so they can take time to meditate.

To incorporate mindful meditation into your life, follow these steps:

1. Find a quiet place where you won't be interrupted. You want to focus on your meditation and not the noise that is

going on inside of your home. Some people like to play meditation music to help drown out any noise around their homes. But you don't want to play the music too loudly as this can distract you when you are trying to meditate.

2. Find a comfortable spot to sit or lie down. The key is to be comfortable so you can focus on your thoughts and not the fact that your leg is falling asleep or you are starting to feel uncomfortable.

3. You want to keep your body straight, but you don't want to become too stiff. Ensure that your spine's natural curvature is there, as this will keep you comfortable and focused on the task.

4. Ensure your arms are parallel to your upper body. You can rest your hands on the top of your legs.

5. Some people like to close their eyes while others will keep their eyes open. If you keep your eyes open, don't focus on one object.

6. Start to focus on your breathing. Begin by breathing normally. Notice how your body feels when you inhale and exhale.

7. After you become more relaxed, take a few deep and slow breaths, which will help your body completely relax.

8. Some people like to "follow" their breath. This means they visualize air going in and out of their bodies. Some people take this a bit farther and imagine any negative energy leaving their body when they exhale and positive energy entering their body when they inhale.
9. At some point, your mind will stop focusing on your breathing, and you will start thinking random thoughts. For example, you might think about what you need to do that day, what you need to pick up at the grocery store, how you need to prepare the evening meal, what activities your children have that day, etc.
10. Acknowledge every thought, and then let it leave your mind. The key is to start focusing on your thoughts.
11. Every minute or so, you should turn your attention back to your breathing, as this will keep you from focusing on a thought too long.

Once you are done meditating, gently start to bring yourself back into the motions of the room. You can focus on an item or listen to the noise that is happening inside of your home. You want to bring yourself out of your haze gently, so you don't feel rushed. You want to hold on to that calm feeling as long as possible.

Chapter 9: Change Your Habits

You might be surprised how the tips you have just read about have changed from the psychological ones people haven't been doing before, such as meditation, to those you have always known, such as eating, sleeping, and exercising. The point is that when people start to focus on success, they tend to lose sight of the basics, such as eating and sleeping right. People tend to focus more on what will give them the biggest success and less on the fundamentals that will help them maintain a healthy mindset.

It is important always to follow the four principles of a healthy lifestyle, no matter where you are in your self-discipline mastery. These four principles will help you stay focused on the tasks and give you the best chances of success. The four principles are:

1. **Drinking right.** You want to drink at least two liters of water or eight 8oz glasses every day. While you can drink milk and other fluids throughout your day, water is the most important.

2. **Eating healthy.** Not only should you focus on eating more healthy fats, but you also need to make sure you get enough fruits, vegetables, and other food groups.
3. **Getting enough sleep.** As an adult, you should get at least seven hours of good sleep every night, though many doctors state getting eight is better.
4. **Exercising.** You don't need to exercise for two hours every day, but you should set aside at least half an hour to exercise throughout your day. The least amount of time you should exercise twice a week is 20 minutes. For instance, one of the best exercises you can take part in is going for a 20-minute walk.

For most people, the hardest part of developing self-discipline is changing their habits. Fortunately, the more consistent you are with your new habits, the easier they are to change. In reality, it only takes a few days to a week to get into better habits, as long as you are consistent and remain focused on your habit.

One of the ways to change an unhealthy habit is to replace it with a healthier habit. For example, if you find yourself snacking on chips throughout the day, you can change your snack to something healthier, such as carrots, apples, or oranges. If you struggle to get to bed at a decent time and do not get enough sleep throughout the night, get up earlier in the morning. This will make you more tired at the end of the day, and you will find yourself going to bed earlier.

Always remember to talk to yourself compassionately when you are focusing on change. If you don't follow through with your change one day, don't become frustrated with yourself. Forgive yourself and get in the mindset that tomorrow is a new day.

If you know that your unhealthy habits result from stress, you need to find ways to decrease some of your stress, as this will help you stay more focused on healthy habits. Sometimes eliminating stress is a mindset change. You need to look at stress as an avenue for growth and opportunity instead of work that must be done. Other times, you need to make some other lifestyle changes to help yourself decrease your stress.

Conclusion

By now, you might feel that your mind is overloaded with various tips and strategies to help you become a master of self-discipline. It is important not to let all this information overwhelm you. Remember that you will take everything step by step, and you can go as slow as you need to. As people often say, slow and steady wins the race!

The contents of this book not only help you learn what self-discipline is, but you also learn how to improve your self-discipline. You know the difference between self-esteem and self-confidence and how each tie into self-discipline. You know how to meditate, become more mindful, and focus on changing your habits by replacing unhealthy habits with healthy ones. You also understand that you need to control your mind by maintaining focus.

Some of the key points from this book you need to remember every day is as follows:

- Always compassionately speak to yourself. You should give yourself the same respect and care that you give your best friend. If you wouldn't say something to someone else, why would you say it to yourself? Don't put yourself

down by letting your inner critic take control.
- Working toward mastering your self-discipline will be draining. There are times you will feel exhausted and not sure you can continue. Take a break and allow yourself time to breathe. Then, continue focusing on your plan and reaching your goal.
- Never be afraid of failure. Fall forward and allow failure to help you grow.
- Learn from your mistakes and move on.
- Always remember that 'no' is a sentence all by itself. You do not have to give people a reason why you can't take on extra work.
- Put yourself first, as your mental and emotional health is important.
- Always take time to ensure you have some 'me time' during your day, as this will help you maintain a calm environment.
- Use the SMART rule when creating goals and write down your goals. Make sure that you have little steps to help you reach your goals.
- Remember that learning is a constant part of your life. If you are smart, you will never stop learning.

No matter what you do, never give up. You are a strong person, and you will succeed in your mission to become a master of self-discipline.

I hope you have enjoyed this book. For me, there is no greater reward than your satisfaction.

If you liked this book, I´d appreciate it if you could take a couple of minutes to leave a review on Amazon.

Thank you.
G. Hill

References

400 Positive Quotes That Will Make Your Day Wonderful. Retrieved 3 November 2019, from
https://wisdomquotes.com/positive-quotes/

A quote from The Subtle Art of Not Giving an F*ck. Retrieved 2 November 2019, from
https://www.goodreads.com/quotes/8678550-at-some-point-most-of-us-reach-a-place-where

B., O. 27 Powerful Quotes to Boost Your Self Confidence | Code of Living. Retrieved 1 November 2019, from
https://www.codeofliving.com/27-powerful-quotes-to-boost-your-self-confidence/

Chua, C. (2019). How to Stop Procrastinating: 11 Practical Ways for Procrastinators. Retrieved 3 November 2019, from
https://www.lifehack.org/articles/featured/11-practical-ways-to-stop-procrastination.html

Crockett, R. (2019). The Growth Mindset Choice: 10 Fixed Mindset Examples We Can Change. Retrieved 1 November 2019, from
https://www.wabisabilearning.com/blog/fixed-mindset-examples

Dunn, C. (2019). 10 Things You Can Do to Boost Self-Confidence. Retrieved 3 November 2019, from
https://www.entrepreneur.com/article/281874

Edberg, H. (2019). 27 Smart and Simple Ways to Motivate Yourself. Retrieved 4 November 2019, from
https://www.positivityblog.com/motivate-yourself/

Fixed Mindset vs. Growth Mindset: What REALLY Matters for Success. (2019). Retrieved 1 November 2019, from https://www.developgoodhabits.com/fixed-mindset-vs-growth-mindset/

Garcy, P. (2015). 9 Reasons You Procrastinate (and 9 Ways to Stop). Retrieved 2 November 2019, from https://www.psychologytoday.com/us/blog/fearless-you/201506/9-reasons-you-procrastinate-and-9-ways-stop

Golden Rules of Goal Setting: Five Rules to Set Yourself Up for Success. Retrieved 1 November 2019, from https://www.mindtools.com/pages/article/newHTE_90.htm

Griggs, S. (2018). 11 Tips to Master Self-Discipline and Rid Yourself of Bad Habits. Retrieved 2 November 2019, from https://startupnation.com/start-your-business/tips-self-discipline-bad-habits/

How to Practice Mindfulness Meditation - Mindful. (2019). Retrieved 4 November 2019, from https://www.mindful.org/mindfulness-how-to-do-it/

Klint, L. Learning is living: Making knowledge a priority. Retrieved 1 November 2019, from https://www.pluralsight.com/blog/career/making-learning-priority

Loveless, B. 12 Strategies to Motivate Your Child to Learn. Retrieved 2 November 2019, from https://www.educationcorner.com/motivating-your-child-to-learn.html

Meah, A. 36 Inspirational Quotes On Self-Discipline | AwakenTheGreatnessWithin. Retrieved 1 November 2019, from
https://www.awakenthegreatnesswithin.com/36-inspirational-quotes-on-self-discipline/

Morin, A. (2015). 7 Reasons You Need Mental Strength to Be Successful. Retrieved 2 November 2019, from
https://www.success.com/7-reasons-you-need-mental-strength-to-be-successful/

Patel, D. (2019). 10 Powerful Ways to Master Self-Discipline. Retrieved 1 November 2019, from
https://www.entrepreneur.com/article/287005

Patel, N. (2016). 7 Brain Hacks to Improve Your Focus at Work. Retrieved 4 November 2019, from
https://www.forbes.com/sites/neilpatel/2016/08/12/7-brain-hacks-to-improve-your-focus-at-work/#509ebdf959a8

Rice, A. (2006). Urban Dictionary: Scarlett O'Hara. Retrieved 2 November 2019, from
https://www.urbandictionary.com/define.php?term=Scarlett%20O%27Hara

Ten Ways to Avoid Temptation and Improve Self-Discipline. Retrieved 2 November 2019, from
https://www.equitybank.com/your-life/ten-ways-to-avoid-temptation-and-improve-self-discipline

Truex, L. (2019). How to Create an Action Plan to Achieve Your Home Business Goals. Retrieved 1 November 2019, from
https://www.thebalancesmb.com/how-to-create-an-action-plan-to-achieve-your-goals-1794129

What is mental toughness? - Mental Toughness Inc. Retrieved 3 November 2019, from **http://www.mentaltoughnessinc.com/what-is-mental-toughness/**